Contents

The origins of the war

On 28 June 1914 in the Bosnian capital, Sarajevo, a teenager called Gavrilo Princip shot dead the heir to the Austro-Hungarian throne, Archduke Franz Ferdinand, and his wife Sophie. This act marked a turning-point in world history for it sparked off a whole series of events that led to war. The First World War (1914-18) claimed the lives of nearly 10 million soldiers. The horror and misery of those caught up in this terrible conflict are almost unimaginable, but one way to gain a sense of what they had to endure is to read the poetry written during the war.

Some of the writers featured in this book were poets before they went to fight, for example Isaac Rosenberg and Edward Thomas (see page 15). Others turned to poetry during the fighting as a much-needed means of expression. Some, such as the women poets in this book, were not involved directly in the fighting yet still had to deal with hardships at home. Several of the poets discussed were also journalists, artists and musicians. Many were killed during the conflict.

> **❝** We are the Dead. Short days ago
> We lived, felt dawn, saw sunset glow,
> Loved and were loved, and now we lie
> In Flanders fields. **❞**
>
> From 'In Flanders Fields' by John McCrae

Archduke Franz Ferdinand and his wife Sophie in the Bosnian capital, Sarajevo, shortly before their assassination on 28 June 1914. The Archduke had decided to visit Sarajevo even though he had been warned of the dangers of the situation in Bosnia-Herzegovina (see page 7).

The balance of power

Why did Princip step out of the crowd of demonstrators around the Archduke's carriage with a gun in his hand on that fateful day in 1914? To understand what happened then and afterwards, it is necessary to look back at events towards the end of the 1800s.

Throughout much of the 19th century, countries in Europe maintained a balance of power that helped to prevent wars involving more than two or three countries. However, one war that did break out was a conflict between France and Prussia (a German state). This war ended in 1871 with victory for the Prussians, and the creation of a unified Germany. Many of the other European countries grew increasingly uneasy and fearful about this powerful newcomer, with its industrial might and well-trained armies. Countries in

Poets of the First World War

Nicola Barber and Patrick Lee-Browne

Published by Evans Brothers Limited
2A Portman Mansions
Chiltern Street
London W1M 1LE

VISIT OUR WEBSITE
www.evansbooks.co.uk

First published 2001
Printed by Oriental Press, Dubai, U.A.E

British Cataloguing in Publication Data
Barber, Nicola
    Poets of the first world war. - (Writers in Britain)
    1. World War, 1914-1918 - Poetry 2. War poetry, English -
    History and criticism - 20th century
    I. Title
    821.9'12'080358

    ISBN 023752239X

This book is dedicated to Martin.

Acknowledgements

Consultant – Adrian Barlow

Editor – Nicola Edwards
Designer – Mark Holt
Production – Jenny Mulvanny

For permission to reproduce copyright material, the authors and publishers gratefully acknowledge the following:

Cover: (background) British Library Reproductions (left) Hulton Getty (top right) Topham Picturepoint (bottom right) Topham Picturepoint **page 3:** The Imperial War Museum **page 5:** (left) Hulton Getty (centre) Topham Picturepoint (right) Gloucestershire County Library Service, Gloucestershire Collection **page 6:** Topham Picturepoint **page 7:** (top) The British Library (bottom) Hulton Getty **page 8:** (top) Topham Picturepoint (bottom) Topham Picturepoint **page 9:** (top) Topham Picturepoint (bottom) Hulton Getty **page 10:** (top) Louvre, Paris/Bridgeman Art Library (bottom) JS Library International **page 11:** Topham Picturepoint **page 12:** Topham Picturepoint **page 13:** (top) Hulton Getty (middle) Hulton Getty (bottom) Topham Picturepoint **page 14:** (top) Gloucestershire County Library Service, Gloucestershire Collection (bottom) Hulton Getty **page 15:** (top) By courtesy of the National Portrait Gallery, London (bottom) Hulton Getty **page 16:** (top) Hulton Getty (bottom) Hulton Getty **page 17:** Topham Picturepoint **page 18:** (top) The Imperial War Museum (bottom) Topham Picturepoint **page 19:** Topham Picturepoint **page 20:** (top) Topham Picturepoint (bottom) Topham Picturepoint **page 21:** (top) Topham Picturepoint) (bottom) Hulton Getty **page 22:** Topham Picturepoint **page 23:** (top) The Harry Ransom Centre, University of Texas (bottom) Topham Picturepoint **page 24:** Gloucestershire County Library Service, Gloucestershire Collection **page 25:** (top) The Imperial War Museum (bottom) Topham Picturepoint **page 26:** (top) Hulton Getty (bottom) Topham Picturepoint **page 27:** (top) The British Film Institute (bottom) Hulton Getty

'Landscapes with Figures 2' from *Keith Douglas: Complete Poems*, edited by Desmond Graham, published in 1978 by Oxford University Press

Europe also competed for colonies overseas, scrambling to bring territories in Africa and Asia under their control.

As the balance of power altered, some European countries began to form military alliances, promising to help each other in case of attack. Austria-Hungary and Germany signed such an agreement in 1879, joined by Italy in 1882 to form the Triple Alliance. Germany began to build a 'world-class navy' to rival that of Britain. In response, Britain and France formed an agreement in 1904, known as the Entente Cordiale. They were joined by Russia in 1907.

Meanwhile, in 1908, Austria-Hungary annexed (took over by military force) the Balkan state of Bosnia-Herzegovina. However, millions of Slavic people in Bosnia-Herzegovina did not want to live under Austro-Hungarian rule – they wished their country to be part of the neighbouring Slavic kingdom of Serbia, and many Serbians agreed. Secret societies were formed with the aim of driving the Austrians out of Bosnia-Herzegovina. It was one of these societies, known as the 'Black Hand', that provided Gavrilo Princip with the gun with which he shot Archduke Franz Ferdinand.

The manuscript of 'Anthem for Doomed Youth', written by Wilfred Owen (see page 14) in 1917. The alterations on this draft of the poem were made by Siegfried Sassoon, when Owen met his fellow poet at Craiglockhart hospital (see page 15).

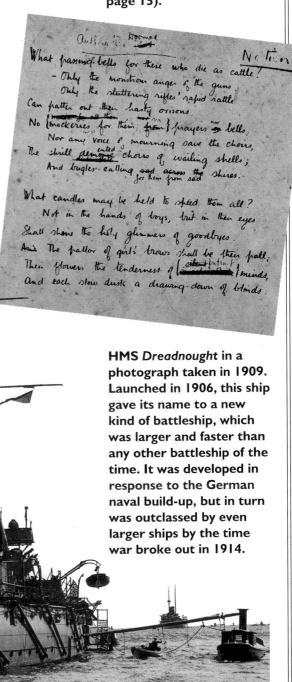

HMS *Dreadnought* in a photograph taken in 1909. Launched in 1906, this ship gave its name to a new kind of battleship, which was larger and faster than any other battleship of the time. It was developed in response to the German naval build-up, but in turn was outclassed by even larger ships by the time war broke out in 1914.

The First World War

Austria-Hungary blamed Serbia for the assassination in Sarajevo. Backed by Germany, it sent a list of demands to Serbia, requiring that Serbia should take action against Serb nationalists. After taking advice from Russia, Serbia agreed to most of these demands. However, Austria-Hungary was determined to use this opportunity to crush the Serbs and, on 28 July 1914, it declared war on Serbia, provoking Russia to mobilise its troops for war. In response, Germany declared war on Russia on 1 August, and on France on 3 August. German troops swept through Belgium, which was neutral, on their way to France. The German invasion of Belgium drew Great Britain into the conflict: it declared war on Germany on 4 August. Most people believed that the war would quickly be over. In fact, it was to last for four years.

BRAVO, BELGIUM!

'Bravo, Belgium!' was published in *Punch* magazine in August 1914. It romanticises the role of plucky little Belgium in opposing the German advance across Europe.

The Western Front

German forces advanced quickly across Belgium and into France. However, the Allies (France and Britain) managed to block their progress in the First Battle of the Marne (September 1914),

Vladimir Ilyich Lenin addresses the people of Moscow after his return to Russia from exile in Switzerland in 1917.

The other fronts

The First World War was fought in many parts of the world. The Eastern Front stretched along the borders between Russia and Germany, and Russia and Austria-Hungary. The fighting continued across this area until 1917, when there was a revolution in Russia. After the revolution, the new Russian leader, V.I. Lenin signed a peace treaty with Germany. Other areas of conflict included Palestine and Mesopotamia (present-day Iraq), the border region between Italy and Austria-Hungary, and Gallipoli (see box page 9).

preventing the Germans from reaching Paris. The Germans then turned towards the English Channel, in an attempt to seize control of the Channel ports. Allied troops moved to cut them off in a series of battles known as the 'Race for the Sea'. The First Battle of Ypres (October-November 1914) finally halted the Germans. By late November the two sides had reached stalemate, with neither side able to make any further ground. Both Allied and German troops dug themselves into defensive ditches called trenches. Soon, these systems of trenches marked a battlefront, known as the Western Front, that extended over 700 kilometres from the English Channel to Switzerland.

For the next three years there was deadlock on the Western Front. Both sides launched attacks from their trenches, killing thousands of troops but making little ground. For example, on the first day of the Battle of the Somme (July 1916) there were over 60,000 British casualties (see page 18). When the last attack in this battle was finally called off in November, the Allies had gained just 11 kilometres.

The end

In 1917, the USA entered the war on the side of the Allies. By the end of the war almost 2 million US troops were fighting in Europe, and it was partly this boost in manpower that helped the Allies to win the war. The Second Battle of the Marne (July-August 1918) was a vital victory for the Allies and marked a turning-point in the war. The Germans finally agreed to sign an armistice in November 1918. The fighting stopped at 11 o'clock, on the 11th day of the 11th month. The First World War was over.

An artist's impression of the sinking of the *Lusitania*. This passenger ship was sunk by a German submarine on 7 May 1915. The incident increased American support for the British war effort.

Gallipoli

In October 1914 the Ottoman (Turkish) Empire entered the war on the side of the Central Powers (Germany and its allies). The Turks closed the sea route that led from the Aegean Sea to the Black Sea, blocking the Allies' supply line to southern Russia. Allied troops were sent to the Gallipoli Peninsula, at the western end of the narrow sea route, in April 1915. But the campaign was a disaster, and the Allies were forced to evacuate in December. There were about 250,000 Allied casualties, including many troops from Australia and New Zealand who played a large part in the Gallipoli campaign.

Troops land at Anzac Cove on the Gallipoli Peninsula in 1915.

War poetry

This cup, known as the Douris Cup, was made in ancient Greece in about 490BC and depicts a scene from the Trojan War. With the aid of the goddess of warfare, Athena, one of the greatest Greek warriors of the war, Ajax (left), attacks the Trojan, Hector (right).

War is one of the oldest subjects for poetry. As early as 900BC the Greek poet Homer described the Trojan War in his epic poem *The Iliad*. The poem spans the ten years of the war from the abduction of Helen by Paris, son of the king of Troy, to the siege of Troy by the Greeks, with such dramatic events as the killing of Hector by Achilles and the eventual sacking of the city through the trick of the wooden horse.

Celebrating bravery

War provided the subject matter for one of the earliest poems in English: *The Battle of Maldon*. This poem was written by an anonymous poet some time in the 11th century. It records a battle between East Saxons living in Essex, led by Earl Byrhtnoth, and a band of invading Vikings:

> *The seafarers hoisted their shields on high*
> *And carried them over the gleaming water.*
> *Byrhtnoth and his warriors awaited them,*
> *Ready for battle . . . The time had come*
> *For all the doomed men to fall in the fight.*

Kenneth Branagh's film version of *Henry V*. In this scene, Henry rouses his exhausted troops before the Battle of Agincourt.

The history of England, including foreign as well as civil wars, was a popular subject for Shakespeare and his contemporaries. Battlefield speeches such as that of Henry V before the Battle of Agincourt drew on the traditional values of honour and bravery:

> *And gentlemen in England, now abed,*
> *Shall think themselves accursed they were not here,*
> *And hold their manhoods cheap whiles any speaks*
> *That fought with us upon Saint Crispin's Day.'*
> From *Henry V* (1598-9) by William Shakespeare

'Some one had blunder'd'

On 25 October 1854 a tactical blunder in the Battle of Balaclava between British and Russian forces during the Crimean War led to the near annihilation of the British cavalry ordered to attack Russian artillery. A report of the attack in *The Times* inspired Alfred Tennyson, then Poet Laureate, to write 'The Charge of the Light Brigade'. The poem is perhaps the best-known of pre-20th century war poems. It is memorable because of its strong rhythms and the powerful imagery that balances the bravery and stupidity of the action:

> 66 *Storm'd at with shot and shell,*
> *Boldly they rode and well,*
> *Into the jaws of Death,*
> *Into the mouth of Hell*
> *Rode the six hundred.* 99

Kipling and the Boer War

Britain fought a large number of wars in defence of its empire throughout the 19th century. The Boer War (1899-1902) was waged against Dutch South African settlers when Britain tried to interfere in the government of Transvaal. Rudyard Kipling was well-known as a patriotic poet, yet some of his poems written in reaction to the Boer War were critical of the conflict:

'*Here, where the senseless bullet fell,*
And the barren shrapnel burst,
I will plant a tree, I will dig a well,
Against the heat and the thirst.'

From 'The Settler'

It is only really in the last hundred years that poetry has become a voice of opposition to war. In the 20th century, armies were made up of men who had been well-educated and could read and write. This, together with improved methods of communication, meant that the people who were actually fighting the battles could not only write about their experiences but have them published while the war was going on. From the Boer War (see box) onwards, war poetry became increasingly critical of conflict, and such poetry remains a feature of the writing of our own times. For example, contemporary poets such as James Fenton and Tony Harrison have written powerful poems responding to conflicts in Vietnam and the Gulf.

Burning oil refineries in Kuwait in 1991. They were set on fire by Iraqi troops retreating at the end of the Gulf War (1990-1). Tony Harrison's poem 'The Gaze of the Gorgon' was written in 1992 for a television programme and traces the horror of war from Troy to the Gulf.

Patriotism

The outbreak of war in August 1914 inspired many writers and poets to put pen to paper in support of the war. A group of the most influential authors of the day was assembled by the British government to back Britain's fight against Germany; among those involved were Sir Arthur Conan Doyle, H. G. Wells and Thomas Hardy. In the early months of the war *The Times* published a number of poems celebrating the fact that Britain was fighting for a just cause (since Germany had declared war and invaded Belgium illegally; see page 8) while also acknowledging that many of the men setting off for France would not return.

Thomas Hardy published a number of poems in support of the war effort. He held many reservations about war in general, but was resigned to the need to resist Germany's aggression. His poem 'Men who March Away' captures the mood of regret and determination:

> " *In our heart of hearts believing*
> *Victory crowns the just,*
> *And that braggarts must*
> *Surely bite the dust,*
> *Press we to the field ungrieving,*
> *In our heart of hearts believing*
> *Victory crowns the just.* "

Other poets writing at this time used a style which recalled the language of the Bible and of religious ceremony. This had the effect of linking war service with religious commitment, so making the war a spiritual battle as well as a physical one:

> " *Through joy and blindness he shall know,*
> *Not caring much to know, that still*
> *Nor lead nor steel shall reach him, so*
> *That it be not the Destined Will.* "
>
> From 'Into Battle' by Julian Grenfell

'I hate not Germans...'

Some writers were quick to react against the general mood of excited enthusiasm. Edward Thomas (see page 15) was among those who pressed for a more balanced view of the war:

'*This is no case of petty right or wrong*
That politicians or philosophers
Can judge. I hate not Germans, nor grow hot
With love of Englishmen, to please newspapers.'

From 'This is No Case of Petty Right or Wrong'

Edward Thomas

Rupert Brooke

Many of those who wrote enthusiastic and patriotic poems signed up for service in the Army when war broke out. Rupert Brooke was the most conspicuous of these 'soldier poets'. A young man of 26, he had enjoyed great popularity and success at Cambridge University, and had friends in high places such as Winston Churchill and Herbert Asquith, the Prime Minister. In December 1914 he wrote a sequence of five sonnets which linked the war to the nobility and sentimentality of a mythical past. Brooke's most famous poem from this sequence is 'The Soldier'. This sonnet was quoted in a sermon in St Paul's Cathedral by the Dean of St Paul's in April 1915, which indicates the popularity of Brooke's writing, and the degree to which it represented the voice of patriotic Britain.

> *If I should die, think only this of me:*
> *That there's some corner of a foreign field*
> *That is for ever England.*

Rupert Brooke, photographed shortly before his death in 1915 (see page 18). Brooke captured the public imagination with his good looks and the patriotic sentiments of his poetry.

December 1915. Eager recruits queue outside Southwark Town Hall in London to enlist for military service (see page 20).

The Cenotaph war memorial in London

'Age shall not weary them...'

Perhaps the most widely used lines of war poetry were written right at the start of the war. Laurence Binyon's 'For the Fallen' was published in *The Times* on 21 September 1914. The central verse of the poem is often quoted in Remembrance Day services, and on war memorials:

'They shall not grow old as we that are left grow old;
Age shall not weary them, nor the years condemn.
At the going down of the sun and in the morning
We will remember them.'

The First World War poets

The five major First World War poets whose work is discussed throughout this book all fought on the Western Front and experienced the grim realities of trench warfare at first-hand. Their poetry reminds us to this day of, in Owen's words, the 'pity of War'.

Ivor Gurney 1890-1937

Ivor Gurney in a photograph taken in 1915, the year in which he joined the army. He had been rejected in 1914 on account of his poor eyesight.

Gurney was born in Gloucester. As a child, he was a chorister in the Cathedral Choir. In 1911 he went to London, to study at the Royal College of Music. At this time he also began to write poetry. In London, Gurney missed Gloucester and its surrounding countryside, and he began to develop the mental instability that was to dog him for the rest of his life.

Gurney joined up in 1915 and served with the Gloucestershire Regiment. 1n 1916, the Gloucesters were sent to the front line near Ypres, then moved to the Somme for the final month of the offensive there (see page 19). In 1917, Gurney was wounded and gassed, and was sent back to Britain to recover. In the same year, his first book of poetry, *Severn and Somme* was published. It was followed by *War's Embers* in 1919.

After the war, Gurney resumed his studies at the Royal College of Music. But his eccentric behaviour and threats of suicide led to his being admitted to a mental asylum, where he remained until his death in 1937.

Wilfred Owen 1893-1918

Owen was born in Oswestry, Shropshire. He spent some time teaching in France before the war, but returned to Britain in 1915 to join up. In 1916, he found himself in the front line, serving with the Manchester Regiment. He was gassed, and in the bitter weather of winter 1916-17 was forced to sleep outside in the snow. He wrote to his mother: 'The marvel is that we did not all die of cold. As a matter of fact, only one of my party actually froze to death...' He also began to write poetry about his experiences.

In 1917, suffering from shell-shock (see page 23), Owen was sent to Craiglockhart War Hospital, in Edinburgh. There he met the poet Siegfried Sassoon who encouraged him with his writing. Owen returned to the trenches in 1918, winning a Military Cross for his bravery. He was killed on 4 November. His parents received the news of his death as the bells rang out in Shrewsbury on 11 November 1918 to celebrate the signing of the Armistice which ended the war.

Wilfred Owen

Isaac Rosenberg 1890-1918

The son of immigrant Lithuanian Jews, Rosenberg was brought up in Bristol and London. He drew and wrote from an early age, and was apprenticed to an engraver at the age of 14. He studied at the Slade School of Art for two years, all the time continuing to experiment with his poetry.

He joined up in 1915, although he was physically small and frail. In the army he suffered much abuse for this, for his artistic interests, and for his Jewishness. He was sent to France in 1916, and fought on the Somme in the early months of 1917. He was killed on 1 April 1918, aged 27. His body was never found.

Isaac Rosenberg painted a number of self-portraits. This one, dating from 1915, shows him in a felt hat. He enlisted in order to give much-needed financial support to his family.

Siegfried Sassoon 1886-1967

Born in Kent of a wealthy family, Sassoon went to Marlborough College and Cambridge University. He was a keen cricketer and loved fox-hunting. He volunteered in August 1914 and served in the Royal Welch Fusiliers where he met the writer Robert Graves. Despite fighting with great bravery, and winning a Military Cross, Sassoon became disillusioned with the war. In 1917, he was wounded in the shoulder and sent home. It was at this time that he issued a statement arguing for an immediate end to the war: '...I have seen and endured the sufferings of the troops, and I can no longer be a party to prolong these sufferings for ends which I believe to be evil and unjust...' As a result of this protest he went to Craiglockhart hospital (see page 23), where he met Wilfred Owen.

Sassoon returned to fight on the Western Front and survived the war.

Siegfried Sassoon, photographed in the early stages of the war, before he became embittered by his experiences in the trenches

Edward Thomas 1878-1917

Thomas was born and educated in London and Oxford. His family came from Wales and he developed a love of the countryside which is evident in his poetry. He married before he left Oxford University, and struggled to make ends meet as a freelance writer. In 1914 he became friendly with the American poet Robert Frost, who encouraged him to write poetry.

Thomas joined up in 1915 and met Wilfred Owen during his training. He remained in England for 18 months, arriving in France in January 1917. He was killed only three months later, on Easter Monday, on the first day of the Battle of Arras.

'In Memoriam (Easter, 1915)'

'The flowers left thick at nightfall in the wood
This Eastertide call in to mind the men,
Now far from home, who, with their
*   sweethearts, should*
Have gathered them and will do never again.'

15

Over the top

By spring 1915, a line of trenches marked the battlefront between the Allies and the Germans in Western Europe. The trenches nearest the enemy, known as the front line, were connected by communication trenches to 'support' and 'reserve' trenches behind. Separating the two enemy front lines was an area called 'No Man's Land' which varied in width from several thousand metres in some places to just a few metres in others. Rolls of barbed wire in No Man's Land were placed to act as a barrier against attack.

The Germans spent a great deal of time and energy constructing deep, well-built defensive trenches, lined with timber and even with electric light in the deepest, concrete-built dugouts. The Allies, however, saw trenches as a less permanent solution. Their trenches were often little more than water-logged ditches in which men were forced to live in knee-deep mud. Worse, in many places the Allies were forced to dig their defences in low-lying, swampy areas while the Germans took control of higher – and drier – ground. Siegfried Sassoon's first poem written at the front line opens with a description of a trench at night:

German soldiers fire into No Man's Land from their front line trenches. This photograph was taken in 1915.

> 66 *Darkness: the rain sluiced down; the mire was deep;*
> *It was past twelve on a mid-winter night,*
> *When peaceful folk in beds lay snug asleep;*
> *There, with much work to do before the light,*
> *We lugged our clay-sucked boots as best we might*
> *Along the trench; sometimes a bullet sang,*
> *And droning shells burst with a hollow bang;*
> *We were soaked, chilled and wretched, every one;*
> *Darkness; the distant wink of a huge gun.* 99
>
> From 'The Redeemer'

British soldiers sit in a trench waiting for dinner to cook on their stove (bottom left).

Attacks

Both sides mounted attacks from their front line trenches with the aim of capturing the trenches of the enemy, and of gaining ground. In fact, the line of the trenches barely changed over the three-and-a-half years of stalemate on the Western Front, yet the cost in human lives was catastrophic. At the Battle of Loos, for example, in September 1915, Allied troops attacked the German front line. The British soldiers advanced across No Man's Land in orderly lines, walking directly towards the enemy's barbed wire defences. Within minutes, most had been mown down by the German defenders' machine-gun fire. Over 8000 men were killed or wounded in a few hours.

The moment of attack, when soldiers were ordered to move out over the edge of the front line trench into No Man's Land, was known as going 'over the top'. In his poem 'The Show', Wilfred Owen (see page 14) imagined looking down at the battlefield from above, watching lines of men – 'thin caterpillars' – move across the scarred battlefield:

> 66 *My soul looked down from a vague height, with Death,*
> *As unremembering how I rose or why,*
> *And saw a sad land, weak with sweats of dearth,*
> *Gray, cratered like the moon with hollow woe,*
> *And pitted with great pocks and scabs of plagues.*
>
> *Across its beard, that horror of harsh wire,*
> *There moved thin caterpillars, slowly uncoiled.*
> *It seemed they pushed themselves to be as plugs*
> *Of ditches, where they writhed and shrivelled, killed.* 99
>
> From 'The Show'

A moment for reflection

In his poem 'Break of Day in the Trenches', Isaac Rosenberg wonders what a rat, scurrying along the trench, makes of the human predicament in which Rosenberg finds himself:

'The darkness crumbles away.
It is the same old druid Time as ever,
Only a live thing leaps my hand,
A queer sardonic rat,
As I pull the parapet's poppy
To stick behind my ear.
Droll rat, they would shoot you if they knew
Your cosmopolitan sympathies.
Now you have touched this English hand
You will do the same to a German
Soon, no doubt, if it be your pleasure...'

From 'Break of Day in the Trenches'

British troops line up in a shallow trench, ready to go 'over the top'. Barbed wire laid by both sides in No Man's Land was a major obstacle to any advance, even though men were sent out at night to cut the wire before an attack.

Poetry and place

German troops lie dead before the French defences at Verdun. The Battle of Verdun was one of the bloodiest conflicts of the war. The purpose of the German attack was to 'bleed the French to death', but both sides suffered casualties of around 400,000 men.

For many people, names such as Ypres, Gallipoli, Verdun, the Somme and Passchendaele will always be associated with the First World War because these are the places where some of the most famous battles were fought. The war poets experienced the grim reality of several of these punishing campaigns.

The Battle of the Somme, 1916

In late 1915, the British general Douglas Haig became Commander-in-Chief of the British forces on the Western Front. Haig decided to launch a new attack in an area of the Front that had been quiet up to that point – the region around the River Somme in northwestern France.

During 1915, the Germans had taken advantage of the peace in this part of the Front to construct deep and secure trench systems, well fortified with protective wire. Haig planned a massive artillery bombardment lasting a week before the actual attack began. He calculated that this would shatter the Germans' defences – but he was proved disastrously wrong. Despite the huge numbers of shells that landed on the German front lines, when British troops attacked on 1 July 1916 they were wiped out by German machine-gun fire. About 100,000 British soldiers went 'over the top' on that day: 20,000 were killed and a further 40,000 wounded.

The Battle of the Somme was planned by General Sir Douglas Haig, pictured here. Haig also commanded the British forces at the Battle of Passchendaele, where casualties exceeded 300,000 men.

On the way to Gallipoli

Rupert Brooke was part of the naval force heading for Gallipoli in 1915. He died of blood poisoning en route and was buried on the Greek island of Scyros. In his last poem 'Soon to Die', he sees his companions turning to ghosts before his very eyes. Gone is the patriotism of his earlier poetry (see page 13); in this poem he faces the realities of war, and of death.

Both Siegfried Sassoon and his friend Robert Graves (see page 23) were involved in the Battle of the Somme. Sassoon was sent home suffering from 'trench fever' in late July. Graves was wounded so badly that a letter was mistakenly sent to his parents informing them of his death. He also was sent home to recover. Ivor Gurney saw only the end of the Somme campaign. In a letter to a friend, he wrote: 'We suffer pain out here, and for myself it sometimes comes that death would be preferable to such a life...'.

One of the victims of the Somme campaign was an American poet, Alan Seeger, who was serving with the French forces. He was killed by gunfire on 4 July 1916. His poem, 'Rendezvous', is particularly poignant:

> 66 *I have a rendezvous with Death*
> *At some disputed barricade,*
> *When Spring comes back with rustling shade*
> *And apple-blossoms fill the air ...* 99

'The Road from Arras to Bapaume', by C. R. W. Nevinson. Nevinson was one of a number of official war artists sent out to the front line to depict the conditions of war for the public at home. This picture shows the bleak, monotonous landscape of the northern end of the Western Front.

Passchendaele, 1917

The Third Battle of Ypres, usually known as Passchendaele after a village that was completely destroyed during the fighting, started in July 1917. Once again the Allied attack was preceded by a huge artillery bombardment. The shells churned up the ground and destroyed the drainage systems in the fields. But as the Allied attacks began, so did the rain. The battlefield quickly flooded and turned into mud so deep and thick that men drowned in it. Edmund Blunden (see box) survived Passchendaele, and wrote an extended poem vividly reliving its horrors and his own feelings of helplessness. This is its ending:

> 66 *Still wept the rain, roared guns,*
> *Still swooped into the swamps of flesh and blood.*
> *All to the drabness of uncreation sunk,*
> *And all thought dwindled to a moan, Relieve!*
> *But who with what command can now relieve*
> *The dead men from that chaos, or my soul?* 99
>
> From 'Third Ypres'

Edmund Blunden (1896-1974)

Blunden joined the Royal Sussex Regiment in 1915. He fought at the battles of the Somme and Ypres. He suffered from gas poisoning and was awarded the Military Cross for bravery. Most of his poetry, as well as a prose account of his experiences, *Undertones of War* (1928) (see page 27), was written after the war.

The home front

Although the war was fought on the European mainland and further afield, its effects were felt by all those left in Britain, on the 'home front'.

This recruitment poster features the secretary of state for war, Field Marshal Lord Kitchener. Unlike many people, he believed that the war would last some time and so built up a large volunteer force, popularly known as 'Kitchener's army'.

Joining up

In the early days of the war, thousands of men rushed to join up – many were encouraged by their mothers or wives to go and fight. So great was the early enthusiasm for the war that women of the Active Service League presented a white feather to any man apparently fit enough to serve but who had not volunteered.

As the lists of dead and wounded grew longer, and the number of recruits dropped, conscription was introduced in 1916, first for unmarried men, and then for all men up to the age of 41. Some men refused on moral grounds to go and fight. Known as conscientious objectors, they had to prove their case in legal hearings. If they were successful, some were employed as ambulance drivers, but others were sent to labour camps or to prison. In his poem 'A Call to National Service', Thomas Hardy spoke out to all those uncertain where their 'duty' lay:

> *Up and be doing, all who have a hand*
> *To lift, a back to bend. It must not be*
> *In times like these that vaguely linger we*
> *To air our vaunts and hopes; and leave our land*
> *Untended as a wild of weeds and sand...*

During the war, over 900,000 women were employed in munitions work making bullets, shells and other explosive devices needed on the Western Front.

A changing world

One consequence of the outbreak of war was the removal of thousands of men from their usual peace-time jobs. Women, who had long been employed in industries such as textile manufacture, now began to take men's places in traditionally male industries such as munitions factories, shipyards and steelworks, and on the land.

H.D.

Both Hilda Doolittle (or H.D. as she was known) and her husband Richard Aldington (see page 27) were writers and poets. Before and during the First World War they were part of a literary group in London which included the American poet Ezra Pound, as well as D.H. Lawrence and his German wife Frieda. During the war, H.D.'s marriage broke up and her brother was killed in the fighting. Yet her poetry does not 'describe' her experiences and emotions in the direct way of many of the other poems in this book. Instead, H.D. uses the beauty of poetic language itself to demonstrate that there is an alternative to the mechanical destructiveness of war. This is an extract from her poem 'The Tribute' written in 1916:

'... squalor has entered and taken our songs
and we haggle and cheat,
praise fabrics worn threadbare,
ring false coin for silver,
offer refuse for meat...'

'A Battery Shelled' by the British artist P. Wyndham Lewis

Bereavement

Although women did not experience at first-hand the horrors of the trenches, those with friends and relations at the Front had to live from day to day with the fear of receiving a telegram bearing bad news. The author Vera Brittain lost many friends in the First World War, most notably her fiancé Roland Leighton and her brother Edward. She wrote poems in memory of both men; this is the opening of her lament for Roland:

> 66 *Perhaps some day the sun will shine again,*
> *And I shall see that still the skies are blue,*
> *And feel once more I do not live in vain,*
> *Although bereft of You...'* 99

Other women wrote poetry to express their grief not for a single death, but for the loss of a whole generation of men. 'The Falling Leaves' was written in 1915 by Margaret Postgate Cole:

> 66 *Slain by no wind or age or pestilence.*
> *But in their beauty strewed*
> *Like snowflakes falling on the Flemish clay.'* 99

Vera Brittain in the uniform of a volunteer nurse. Like many other nurses she served in France, caring for those injured in the fighting.

21

Pain and protest

As the war progressed, some of the war poets used their writing to express not only their own suffering but also their increasing disillusionment with the war and its aims.

Poems of suffering

Wilfred Owen's first winter in the trenches was a terrible one, as he and his men endured unusually cold weather out in the open (see page 14). He translated some of this experience into the poem 'Exposure':

> 66 *Our brains ache, in the merciless iced east winds that knive us...*
> *Wearied we keep awake because the night is silent...*
> *Low, drooping flares confuse our memory of the salient...*
> *Worried by silence, sentries whisper, curious, nervous,*
> *But nothing happens.* 99

Gas attacks

Gas was first used on the Western Front by the Germans in April 1915. Soon both sides were using various gases including chlorine and 'mustard' gas. The effects of gas were hideous. Owen caught the moment of a gas attack in his poem 'Dulce et Decorum Est':

'GAS! GAS! Quick boys! – An ecstasy of fumbling,
Fitting the clumsy helmets just in time;
But someone still was yelling out and stumbling,
And flound'ring like a man in fire or lime...
Dim, through the misty panes and thick green light,
As under a green sea, I saw him drowning.'

'Gas Attack' by the American war artist John Singer Sargent

Isaac Rosenberg, too, suffered as the bitter winter set in across northern France. But he was determined that he would find artistic expression for this new and terrible experience. From a trench on the Somme he wrote to Laurence Binyon (see page 13): 'I am determined that this war, with all its powers for devastation, shall not master my poeting; that is, if I am lucky enough to come through all right. I will not leave a corner of my consciousness covered up, but saturate myself with the strange and extraordinary new conditions of this life, and it will all refine itself into poetry later on.' Sadly, Rosenberg did not 'come through all right' (see page 15), but his war poems, often hastily scribbled, are powerful and vivid (see pages 17 and 25).

Poems of protest

By 1917, Siegfried Sassoon was convinced that the war should be brought to an immediate end and the slaughter stopped. When he issued 'A Soldier's Declaration' in July 1917 (see page 15) he expected to be court-martialled. However, his friend Robert Graves arranged for Sassoon to attend a medical board which, he knew, would declare Sassoon unfit. Sassoon was sent to Craiglockhart (see page 15) to recover from shell-shock. Nevertheless he continued to rage against the war through his poetry which had grown increasingly bitter and critical of those in charge:

Base Details

“ If I were fierce, and bald, and short of breath,
I'd live with scarlet Majors at the Base,
And speed glum heroes up the line to death.
You'd see me with my puffy petulant face,
Guzzling and gulping at the best hotel,
Reading the Roll of Honour. "Poor young chap,"
I'd say – "I used to know his father well;
Yes, we've lost heavily in this last scrap."
And when the war is done and youth stone dead,
I'd toddle safely home and die – in bed. ”

▲ Sassoon's poem 'Base Details' was written on 4 March 1917 in Rouen, while he was serving on the Western Front with the Royal Welch Fusiliers.

▼ A 'Blighty' was the army term for being invalided back to Britain, either for a period of recovery, or for good.

Like many others returning to England after serving in the trenches, Sassoon found a huge gulf between those who had experienced the realities of warfare and those at home. Letters home and reports of battles were heavily censored, and most people in Britain could not begin to imagine the conditions endured by those fighting at the Front.

Shell-shock

Many men returned home from the trenches both physically and mentally wounded. The effects of constant fear and noise, of shells exploding and gunfire all around, reduced many men to stammering and shaking wrecks. This condition was known as 'shell-shock'. Sassoon evoked the horrors of shell-shock in his 1917 poem 'Repression of War Experience':

'You're quiet and peaceful, summering safe at home;
You'd never think there was a bloody war on!...
O yes, you would... why, you can hear the guns.
Hark! Thud, thud, thud, – quite soft... they never cease –
Those whispering guns – O Christ, I want to go out
And screech at them to stop – I'm going crazy;
I'm going stark, staring mad because of the guns.'

Hidden talents

This letter was written by Ivor Gurney to his close friend Marion Scott on 18 January 1917. After the poem he goes on to thank Miss Scott for a food parcel which was 'tres bon'.

Many of the huge numbers of poems written during the First World War were published, but thousands more remain simply as personal mementoes. Practically, a poem was one of the easiest ways for a soldier to express himself in the atrocious conditions of the trenches – all he needed was a pencil and a notebook. However, for some who found themselves at the Front, music and art remained an important part of their lives.

Gurney the musician

Amazingly, given the conditions in which he was living, Ivor Gurney managed to write four songs while he was in the trenches, including the only musical setting that Gurney ever made of his own poetry – 'Severn Meadows'.

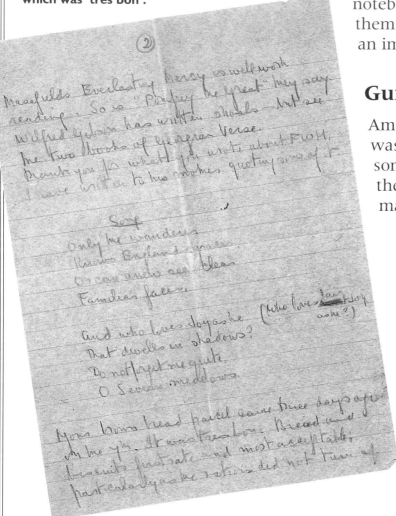

> 66 *And who loves Joy as he*
> *That dwells in shadows?*
> *Do not forget me quite,*
> *O Severn meadows.'* 99
>
> From 'Song'

Music was with Gurney constantly, helping him to maintain his hold on life and sanity. In his poem 'Bach and the Sentry' he describes how playing through a Prelude by J. S. Bach in his mind relieves the tedium and fear of sentry duty (see left). At the end of this poem, Gurney wonders whether memories of the war will ever leave him. In fact, the mental instability already evident before the war (see page 14) became worse in the early 1920s. Gurney was permanently scarred by his war experiences, and he spent the last 15 years of his life in a mental hospital.

Bach and the Sentry

> 66 *Watching the dark my spirit rose in flood*
> *On that most dearest Prelude of my delight.*
> *The low-lying mist lifted its hood,*
> *The October stars showed nobly in clear night.*
>
> *When I return, and to real music-making,*
> *And play that Prelude, how will it happen then?*
> *Shall I feel as I felt, a sentry hardly waking,*
> *With a dull sense of No Man's Land again?* 99

Artists in the trenches

Isaac Rosenberg was an accomplished artist before he joined up in 1915. Some of his fellow students at the Slade School of Art, such as Paul Nash and C.R.W. Nevinson, became offical war artists. Hasty sketches on scraps of paper were all that Rosenberg was able to draw while he was at the Front. In February 1917, Rosenberg wrote to his friend Edward Marsh: 'I've sketched an amusing little thing called 'the louse hunt', and am trying to write one as well...' The poem 'Louse Hunting' summons up a vivid picture of the sight of soldiers, driven mad by lice, burning their clothes and attempting to remove the vermin from their bodies. Rosenberg sees the scene with his artist's eye:

> ❝ *Nudes – stark and glistening,*
> *Yelling in lurid glee. Grinning faces*
> *And raging limbs*
> *Whirl over the floor one fire.*
> *For a shirt verminously busy*
> *Yon soldier tore from his throat, with oaths*
> *Godhead might shrink at, but not the lice...'* ❞

Amateur poets

There were many soldier-poets in the First World War who never had their work published commercially. Their poetry comes down to us in letters and in regimental magazines. They wrote to express their longing for home, their fear, and to remember their dead comrades. Some of their poetry also expresses the ordinary soldier's contempt for those superiors who issued commands from their safe and comfortable quarters, well behind the front lines.

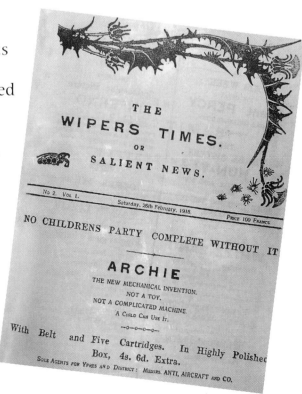

'Back to Billets' by the war artist Eric Kennington. Kennington made many portrait drawings in order to record the 'nameless heroes of the rank and file'. He had served in the army at the start of the war, and preferred to work on his pictures close to the front line.

The *Wipers Times* was a satirical magazine published for the men in the trenches around Ypres. 'Archie', referred to on the cover of this edition, was an army term for German anti-aircraft fire. The magazine included poetry written by the soldiers.

The end and after

The end of the war came on 11 November 1918, but for many life would never be the same again. Many soldiers were permanently maimed and injured, and even those who had escaped serious physical injury had to learn to live with the nightmarish recollections of their experiences during the war. For millions of women left at home, life had to resume without brothers, sons and husbands. A whole generation of men had been lost.

The end of the war was known as the Armistice. The event was celebrated all over Britain by joyful flag-waving crowds such as this.

Poetry after the war

For many, writing continued to be an important part of dealing with the aftermath of war. Edmund Blunden (see page 19) tried to take up studies at Oxford University in 1919 but found it impossible to settle. Instead, he started a successful career in journalism and writing.

Towards the end of his life, Blunden acknowledged that the four years of the 'Great War' never really left him: 'My experiences in the First World War have haunted me all my life and for many days I have, it seemed, lived in that world rather than this.' This extract is taken from Blunden's poem '1916 seen from 1921':

> " *Tired with dull grief, grown old before my day,*
> *I sit in solitude and only hear*
> *Long silent laughters, murmurings of dismay,*
> *The lost intensities of hope and fear...* "

A British war grave cemetery near Ypres, west Flanders, Belgium.

Prose accounts

Many of the soldier-poets published prose accounts of their wartime experiences. Edmund Blunden's *Undertones of War* came out in 1928, followed in 1929 by *Goodbye to All That* by Robert Graves, and *Death of a Hero* by Richard Aldington (see page 21). Once he had begin to recover from the shattering effects of the war, Siegfried Sassoon spent much of the rest of his life reworking his own experiences before and during the war in three books, later collected as *The Memoirs of George Sherston*.

A scene from the film version of *Regeneration* made in 1996, which is based on Pat Barker's novel about the First World War.

Some women writers also recounted their war experiences, notably Vera Brittain in her autobiography *Testament of Youth*, and H.D. (see page 21) in her novel *Bid Me To Live*. Even today, the First World War continues to inspire writers. A recent example is *Regeneration* (1991) by Pat Barker, which deals with Siegfried Sassoon's 'Soldier's Declaration' and his meeting with Wilfred Owen at Craiglockhart War Hospital (see page 15).

The Second World War

The First World War was meant to be the 'war to end wars'. Yet only two decades after the end of the Great War, the world was once again plunged into conflict. The Second World War (1939-45) claimed tens of millions of lives, killing more civilians than soldiers. One of its victims was a British soldier-poet named Keith Douglas. He died in Normandy, three days after the D-Day landings in June 1944. Like Owen and Sassoon before him, Douglas saw the need for poetry to express directly the truth of war. He wrote in a letter to a friend: '...my object... is to write true things, significant things, in words each of which works for its place in the line...' This is the opening of Douglas's poem 'Landscape with Figures 2':

> 66 *On scrub and sand the dead men wriggle*
> *in their dowdy clothes. They are mimes*
> *who express silence and futile aims*
> *enacting this prone and motionless struggle*
> *at a queer angle to the scenery*
> *crawling on the boards of the stage like walls*
> *deaf to the one who opens his mouth and calls*
> *silently...* 99

Robert Graves (1895-1985)

Born in London of an Irish father and a German mother, Graves went straight from school into the Royal Welch Fusiliers. He became friends with both Sassoon and Owen. He fought on the Somme, and in 1929 published an autobiographical account of the war, *Goodbye to All That*.

Robert Graves

HISTORICAL EVENTS		WAR POETS' LIVES
End of Franco-Prussian War; German Empire is established	**1871**	
	1878	Birth of Edward Thomas
Austria-Hungary and Germany sign Dual Alliance	**1879**	
Germany, Austria-Hungary and Italy form Triple Alliance	**1882**	
	1886	Birth of Siegfried Sassoon
	1887	Birth of Rupert Brooke
	1890	Birth of Ivor Gurney Birth of Isaac Rosenberg
	1893	Birth of Wilfred Owen
	1895	Birth of Robert Graves
	1896	Birth of Edmund Blunden
Germany begins to build up naval power	**1897**	
Start of Second Boer War (-1902)	**1899**	
Britain and France sign Entente Cordiale	**1904**	
HMS *Dreadnought* launched	**1906**	
Britain, France and Russia form Triple Entente	**1907**	
Austria-Hungary annexes Bosnia-Herzegovina	**1908**	
	1911	Gurney goes to Royal College of Music Rosenberg goes to Slade School of Art (-1913)
Assassination in Sarajevo of Archduke Franz Ferdinand (28 June) Austria-Hungary declares war on Serbia (28 July) Germany declares war on Russia (1 August) and on France (3 August); German troops invade Belgium Britain declares war on Germany (4 August) First Battle of the Marne (September) First Battle of Ypres (October-November)	**1914**	Sassoon joins up (August) Brooke writes celebrated sequence of five sonnets (December)
Gas first used by Germans on Western Front (April) Gallipoli Campaign (April-December 1915) Sinking of the *Lusitania* (7 May) Battle of Loos (September)	**1915**	Thomas, Rosenberg, Owen and Gurney join up Death of Brooke (23 April)

HISTORICAL EVENTS		WAR POETS' LIVES
Conscription introduced in Britain (January) Battle of Verdun (February-December) Battle of the Somme (July-November)	**1916**	Sassoon and Graves fight in the Battle of the Somme Death of Alan Seeger (4 July) Gurney moves from Ypres to fight in the end of the Battle of the Somme
	1916-17	Owen on the Somme
USA enters the war (6 April) Battle of Arras (April) Battle of Passchendaele (Third Battle of Ypres) (July-November) Russian Revolution (October)	**1917**	Death of Edward Thomas (9 April) Owen sent to Craiglockhart War Hospital, Edinburgh (June) Sassoon issues 'A Soldier's Declaration' (July); he is sent to Craiglockhart War Hospital and meets Owen Blunden fights at Passchendaele (Third Ypres) Publication of *Severn and Somme* by Gurney (October) Sassoon returns to France
Second Battle of the Marne (July-August) Germany signs Armistice to end war (11 November)	**1918**	Death of Rosenberg (1 April) Death of Owen (4 November)
Paris Peace Conference and Treaty of Versailles	**1919**	Publication of *War's Embers* by Gurney Publication of *War Poems* by Sassoon
	1922	Gurney goes into a mental hospital
	1928	Publication of *Undertones of War* by Blunden; *Memoirs of a Fox-Hunting Man* by Sassoon
	1929	Publication of *Goodbye to All That* by Graves; *Death of a Hero* by Richard Aldington
	1930	Publication of *Memoirs of an Infantry Officer* by Sassoon
	1933	Publication of *Testament of Youth* by Vera Brittain
	1936	Publication of *Sherston's Progress* by Sassoon
	1937	Death of Gurney in mental hospital
Second World War	**1939-45**	
	1944	Death of Keith Douglas (June)
	1960	Publication of *Bid Me To Live* by H.D.
	1967	Death of Sassoon
	1974	Death of Blunden
	1985	Death of Graves

Index

Further reading

Good general introductions:

The War Poets: The Lives and Writings of the 1914-18 War Poets by
    Robert Giddings, Bloomsbury
Minds at War: The Poetry and Experience of the First World War by
    David Roberts, Saxon Books

For information about the First World War:

Cambridge Perspectives in History: *The Origins of the First and
    Second World Wars* by Frank McDonough
Evans History in Writing: *The First World War* by Christine Hatt

Websites

http://info.ox.ac.uk/jtap/
(website for First World War poetry, history and other links)

http://www.sjc.ox.ac.uk/graves/graves.html
(Robert Graves Trust)

http://www.wilfred.owen.association.mcmail.com/
(Wilfred Owen Association)

http://www.hcu.ox.ac.uk/jtap/
(Wilfred Owen Multimedia Digital Archive)

http://www.sassoonery.demon.co.uk/
(biography of Sassoon)

http://www.envoy.dircon.co.uk/etf/
(Edward Thomas Fellowship)

http://www.iwm.org.uk/
(Imperial War Museum site)

http://www.worldwar1.com/
(Trenches on the Web)